THE SPACE BETWEEN

By

CORA B. B

DEDICATION

For the quiet places inside me that finally found a voice

— and for the ones who listened when I whispered.

xx

ACKNOWLEDGEMENT

This is a bit like saying thank you at an Oscar Award ceremony. It's really that important to me.

To be able to thank everyone I've been inspired by, every place I've visited, every vision I've had to create this poetry book, has been an inspiration of imagination and love for me.

Special thanks must go to Codsall Writers re: Betty, Maggie and Andie, who are, 'the sense, philosophers, the intelligence of humanity.' (Samuel Beckett) I believe, budding authors and poets should attach themselves to a writers group to spark creativity and allow for valuable, diverse perspective and knowledge. 'No man is an island.' (poet John Donne)

Tettenhall Writers Group led by Jane Seabourne, widely published poet and author. I'm humbled to be in a class with such diverse talent.

Thank you to the coffee shops in Wolverhampton, Ludlow and Barmouth, who have allowed me to soak up inspiration to pen my words. Not forgetting the pubs in Bridgnorth and Wolverhampton, which gave me good vantage points to observe and quench my thirst.

I am grateful for my precious link between Wolverhampton and Ludlow, both hold beauty, inspiration and heritage, which I aspire to share in words with you.

Thank you to my husband Dave, who has helped build the link with my American publisher, Book Prides Publishing, re: Deckard Rhodes and Jason Oliver. And has listened to hours of my poetry readings, this may have driven him to drink!

I received encouragement to share my words with you from many friends and family. My daughters, Louse and Elizabeth and my grandchildren Jack and Taylah, of whom I take my greatest inspiration from.

A last word from William Wordsworth, 'Poetry is the spontaneous overflow of powerful feelings: it takes it's origin from emotion recollected in tranquillity.'

-Cora B B xx

NOTE FROM THE AUTHOR

'We build too many walls and not enough bridges.' by Martin Luther King, junior. Which highlights the need for connection and 'Discipline is the bridge between goals and accomplishment.' (Jim Rohn)

Looking through my poems for this poetry book, I found quite a few with references to bridges in my works. This led me to the title of my book and my link between Wolverhampton and Ludlow. We cross many bridges in life and if you have time to look up metaphors, for bridges, you might see how I have tried to connect – words, bridges, people and ideas.

I hope you enjoy what I wanted to share with you.

\-   Cora B B xx

TABLE OF CONTENTS

Wolverhampton

Wolverhampton streets, some cobbled, some paved,

Old industries still remembered and praised.

Lively market reflect cultural change,

Vast adjustments through decades, wide in range.

Enormous pride in all it holds dear,

Royal visits, Queen Victoria once here.

Heavy industries, faded from sight,

Aerospace and automotive, now take flight.

Molineux roars with fervent cheer,

Preserving the past, while the future draws near.

Town to city, with pride we'll grow,

Out of darkness, the light shall glow.

Never fear change, let progress flow.

In The Piazza

"I tell you, it breaks my heart,

You know what I mean?

All these folks stood here with memories,

Not many young un's,

They filled this piazza yesterday.

On them skateboards they was,

should be stopped.

No respect.

Look, almost eleven o'clock,

Them piazza kids still in bed.

Next year we'll get a big one.

We can carry it between us,

They always let ordinary folks do it,

Well, after all the dignitaries.

Ruby Bates knit my poppy,

Better than them paper ones,

Would you like one next year, Julie?

Only another few minutes, then the bugle will play.

Makes me think of me brother,

He never had time to laze in bed.

Looks lovely, that cascade of poppies,

A full blaze of red."

An emulation of a poem by Alistair McGowan "In the Dry Cleaners," with a Ludlovian accent.

In the Piazza Remembrance Sunday St. Peter's Square, Wolverhampton; with a Midland accent.

Building A Bridge

Life can be a battle,
Struggles, conflicts to solve,
overcoming obstacles, finding
words to convey messages.

Grasp understanding of
others' needs, some are
complex souls with ideas
and thoughts, we need to unfold.

Engage, explore their many needs,
we all have different senses,
like ingredients in a box,
added with care.

The process can be long,
overcoming problems to reach
a destination, is not one man's
journey; search for solutions.

Paint your picture, make it clear,
envisage nature in your edifice,
make melodies on your bridge,
achieve harmonious effects,
to reach the other side.

In The Art Gallery

Psychedelic colours of the sixties,

bathrooms, best rooms,

all would scream,

groovy chicks in PVC.

bright macs.

Even Prince changed

our rain-colour scheme.

Through the glass case,

shone a majestic light,

capturing the stone on

the Indian vase,

Spiritual, powerful,

almost bursting out.

A lord proudly holds

his robe to amaze.

A black eye peeps out

from the plume

of the peacock's feathers;

figs, plums, wild pansy,

and crocus

share the colours in

the rainbow's treasure.

The Space Between

Where does the river of time flow? People, individuals, like objects in the streams and rivers, move along, constantly shifting. A bridge built between two worlds, a symbol of strength, a clock to show the passing of time. Stand or fall upon the simple arch, as bones in our feet. Cross the bridge, seek more. From Queen Street to Castle Street, united through the years.

The newspaper, whispers through these walls, deadlines to meet, gossip filling the air. Echoes from the past: gas-lit streets, barefoot urchins earning a penny or two. Winter smog filling their lungs, sulphurous fumes from Black Country foundries prevailing through the town. Horses galloping to the station, hooves flicking sparks from the cobbles. The chase was on, a train to meet, news hot off the press.

Where quills once scratched, technology moves us on. Roaring presses, click-clacking of Linotype machines, silence now of a computer screen. Castle Street took over the buzz: off the press to publishing, to drivers waiting in the loading bay, engines revving, ready to deliver to newspaper shops. Paper sellers on every corner, catching folks eagerly seeking the news of the day. "Extra! Extra! Read all about it! Express and Star! Express and Star!"

Saturday night, more intense pressure, double whammy, The Pink, Sports Edition, men waiting patiently. Reporters returning with another scoop. It all happened down Castle Street.

Today, the demise of the newspaper brings sadness to the people. News appears on our phones, instant access, that's the way it goes. Today's news is tomorrow's chip paper. Alas, no more newsprint allowed on your chips. Yet opportunities now for change: **SPACE** in the old canteen, same place, new space and a safe place.

SPACE to develop, to bring the vibrations back. Embrace the changes, follow the bridge, move from the old world into **SPACE**, embracing the past.

Penny for Your Life

With apprehension, new hope, and excitement,

He kissed his mother goodbye at the door,

Kitchener's words rang loud in his head,

"Your Country Needs You!" for this great war.

With pals he marched from Tower Street,

looking for a new adventure,

leaving behind poverty and deprivation.

No white feather for him and his pals.

Spirits high, they stuck together,

for their country they'd fight with pride,

taking on the other side.

Lives controlled by the army,

men from every walk of life.

For many, the first time they'd left their homes.

Comradeship grew as they trained at Aldershot,

some billeted in old schools.

PT, mock battles, bayonet and rifle drills,

learning military discipline,

then off to join their regiment.

Waved off once more from coastal ports,

patriotic civilians wished them well.

Looking toned and healthy,

exercise and army food,

they went from boy to man.

Off to France he went,

to face heavy artillery fire.

"Sticky Trench," trapped inside,

Germans shelled the trenches.

Rain continuous, waist-deep in mud,

no sleep for days, no bed to lay their head.

Pioneers arrived to repair,

salvaging what they could, declaring

"Impossible task."

Then withdrew, and left the mess.

The days were never-ending,

the nights cold and dark,

Singing kept them going,

to lighten their hearts

Life came to a swift end

for the "Die-Hards," who fought

for King and Country.

The Battle of Loos took many lives.

"Our George" was one of the best.

Only a penny was given

for what her son had done.

(Remembered With Honors George Edward Barlow, Wolverhampton. 1891
4th November 1915)

The Room

Shall I compare thee to a room I once knew?

A room so still and hushed.

Fact and fiction filled the shelves,

so much knowledge too,

where children ran up to the door and suddenly,

imaginatively, removed their shoes.

"Shush! Do not make a sound,

you're here for one thing!"

Believe me, we knew not to horse around.

The smell lingers now new books,

old books, leather-bound and thick.

An old shiny desk, neat and tidy,

always very slick.

Lavender polish must have been her trick.

Efficiently and skillfully, she removed the

card from each book, placed it

alphabetically in her narrow file,

firmly pressed her stamper into the ink pad

and meaningfully stamped your books.

"One, two, three, four, five," she counted out loud,

looked over her spectacles and gave

one of her looks.

Not very welcoming, I could honestly say,

but I treasure the knowledge

I found to this day.

There is no comparing when I look back today.

I've come for a chat and a book I might take back,

not too many new ones the old ones are tatty.

But now I've got time, I can reserve me a space,

go online and order my bargain from Amazon.

It's all very different today,

children are singing rhymes,

they have a story and play.

The writers' group is laughing,

the librarian's making them tea.

Who's put the puzzles out?

What a happy library.

Morning Dew

He walks his greyhound,
around the lake.
Fishermen give a nod,
he's been there before,
dog knows not to
make a sound.

Morning dew
lies on the ground,
trees hold their autumn
colours; spiders' webs glisten
in the October sun.
Hearts connect
in his favourite rendezvous.

Glassy surface for reflection,
he seeks inner peace,
the stillness below,
like a deep reservoir,
keeps his memories aflow.
Feelings arise and pass,
searching for connection.
In this café by the lake,
he welcomes family
and friends, warm-hearted,
feeling her embrace.

I Will Survive

Ah'm off on a mission, an' leavin' the car,

Ah'm tekin' the bus it ay too fer,

Yer won't believe it, lived 'ere seventy year,

But niver once stepped foot in the Combermere.

Ah gets on the Number One, flash me pass wi' pride,

Butterflies kickin' about inside.

The door swings open, ah see it clear,

Big bold letters, THE COMBERMERE.

Ring the bell, off ah hop, smellin' the beer,

First stop, half a bitter cool an' clear,

Ah bide me time, tek a glance or two,

Wait till no one's lookin', got summat to do.

See, ah'm a wench, an' ah needs a peep,

At the gents' latrine, a secret's deep.

Ah slip in quiet, after a bloke called Ned,

Camera ready, nerves in me yed.

Ah cor believe what ah sees in there,

Roots shootin' up, right from underground,

Straight through the floor, through roof an' all,

Like nature 'ad broke through brick an' wall.

Click goes me camera, a right good shot,

A tree in a bog, who would've thought!

Back at the bar, ah ask the gaffer, "What tree's this then?"

"Who knows? Always growd on that spot."

Ned, smilin' smug, comes over wi' glee,
"Everyone knows, it's a Laver tree!"
So believe it or not, it's plain to see,
That magic bog still grows its tree.

The council, the brewery they all agree,
To tend to that strange old Laver tree.
So next time yer passin', tek a peek inside,
A legend grows, wi' roots spreadin' wide.

(The tree at The Combermere Pub Wolverhampton)

Cup Cakes Lane

Wish you were here,
in this old familiar place,
sharing coffee and a tea cake,
always so full of cheer.

Mulling over memories,
they should be in a book,
some happy, some sad,
the ROF story still told.

Tales of growing up,
living in the
country,
hiding boots in Sunny Gutter,
to change and walk to school
I darna interrupt.

Boxing Day wedding,
you said with a smile,
the florist died the day before,
the photographer lost the film,
oh, where was this heading?

As tales grew and time flew by,
my memories would never
disappear. I look around you're not
there.
I smile to myself
oh, I wish you were here.

Looking Up High Street
(From The Window At Falcon)

O n the corner of Doctor's Lane, a man with a cloth cap comes out of The Fosters Arms, lights his fag. Four ladies amble past from the Antique Centre, give cloth cap a smile, show respect. The Vine Inn hangs a bunch of grapes, man in tee shirt steps outside to vape, tee shirt matches grapes. Pizza van arrives, parks on yellow lines, unloads and delivers to shop the other side – trusting, by leaving van door open. Three painters and decorators, all in white, talk to man with snowy hair. Mother hustles her boys into Men 2 Room, barbers, baby on hip. Cars move freely, heading home from work, or another story to be told? Some heading for The Hermitage or the park by the Severn? Children with headphones manage to chat while listening to the latest rap. Union Jack flying from a lamppost, patriotic. 4×4 turns right into Parlours Hall Hotel, sprightly lady with cockapoo dodges traffic to get to pharmacy.

I sip another drink, decide what to eat: Thali food is very nice, aromatic flavours to indulge, right up my street. The bar is busy, locals doing early doors, atmosphere vibrant, sitting in the window, my favourite place of all. Mates say goodbye: "Good luck to Half Sovereign at Ludlow tomorrow, shame your missus's horse got lame."

On Dinham Bridge

Standing on Dinham Bridge,

feel the river's pulsing muscle beneath your feet.

Teme River strength, as it fights through existence,

encountering obstacles, as we do in life

and people we meet.

Wild, exhilarating, edged with danger.

Above, Ludlow Castle rises like a vision in the sky,

eternally observing with a watchful eye.

Children paddling, laughter echoing excitedly they cry.

Millennium Green, to take your ease,

while contemplating the Donkey Steps.

The horseshoe weir flows freely,

silver mane tumbling downstream,

wondering what comes next.

Wait for spring see salmon leap like a spark

of hope; be patient, you might spot an otter or two,

a kingfisher bright plumage, yellow and blue,

a heron frozen in time fills you with life anew.

Stroll along the Bread Walk, Victorian

riverside promenade, take in the beauty all around.

Another day, climb Whitcliffe, view from that height,

as if an old postcard; beauty found.

From The Turret

What can I see? I see the rolling Clee,
panoramic scenes unfurl,
the Bread Walk, Whitcliffe Hill,
flora and fauna, the ancient town wall
proud and tall; historical buildings,
each send a thrill.

What can I hear? I hear the bellow,
rumbling, booming, tempest River Teme;
the circling, swooping hawks flying high,
their steam-whistle pitch, their scream.

What can I smell? My nostrils twitch,
as aromas of gastronomical delights
fill the air, pines of Mortimer Forest,
hops and malt, Ludlow Brewery cheer,
sweet candy floss from the lively fair.

What can I taste? A town well-seasoned,
rich and wide, its flavours stir my soul,
memories to keep.
Taste the musty ancient walls, stained
with the passage of time, stories deep.

What can I feel? I feel the strength

of the castle stone, the roughness on my hands.

Bond between castle and church,

uniting a town, the beating heart

of a young prince still whispers through

this noble land.

Stately Reverence

Leave behind the tales of Corve Street,
whispering echoes beneath your feet.
Enter through the Clive Arch gateway,
where time grows still,
bucolic charm awaits.

Stately sycamores rustle in the
summer breeze; wildflowers bloom
in careless grace, enticing honey bees.
Atmospheric, idyllic serenity,
quietly sit, experience this infinity.

Birds and butterflies grasp onto ivy
and brambles, entwined on historical
stones, holding records from the past,
all but the paupers, hidden
beneath the paths.

Let your thoughts grow soft and free;
now take the winding path to Linney.

Home

Home is where my heart is,
not where I was born.
It's the home my mother's
roots are the place she
loved so dear.

She showed me so much
when I was young,
the place she grew up:
castle, hills, cobbled lanes,
the woods and riverbanks.

I love to go back now
and follow her gentle voice.
I still stop and listen
to church bells chime,
the river's rasping roar.

This is my home wandering
down Linney, roaming over
Whitcliffe, breathing in the views,
soaking up the friendship,
my Ludlow town.

Toast to Mum

We waited in the silence of the room, holding emotions together.

A basket of flowers ready, in full bloom.

The old familiar clock ticked loudly in the stillness.

In unison, we checked our watches by its chimes.

Someone had lit a fire in the grate, she would have liked that.

The room filled with the smell of freshly toasted bread,

We all looked up and smiled, seeing the same picture:

she was still there, holding the long fork, toasting our bread for

supper.

A knock at the door it was time to go and say goodbye.

Living In The Shadow

At Ludlow Fair where castles rise,
beneath the town's misty skies,
there lived a lass with eyes of blue
Elizabeth Charmer; her stories come true.

With raven hair in braided thread,
she walked where ancient poets tread.
Along the Teme's meandering shore,
tales from village folks about the fallen whore.

A fishmonger's daughter, proud yet kind,
with clever hands and thoughtful mind,
she stitched and sewed by candlelight,
with hands made raw from prison life.

Hand-me-down cloth from the women's mission,
her children walked without suspicion,
They held their heads high,
proud in their mother's eye.

A nobleman's son once sought her grace,
entranced by voice and angel face.
Elizabeth saw through his disguise;
anger and rage made her despise.

On market days she'd often sing,
of summer's bloom and vernal spring,
Even gruff old traders knew,
that Charmer's song could charm them too.

They whispered tales, they shared her pain,
of gypsy blood and noble name,
how fortunes might await;
Elizabeth knew this was not her fate.

Still yearning for the love, who was no more,
who was forced to return to Irish shores,
she built her family fair and strong,
keeping them in her shadow, where they belong.

So she remained in Ludlow's fold,
her spirit bright, her gaze still bold,
a woman wrought of soil and sun,
whose life was tragic, yet still not done,

When the bells of Ludlow ring,
listen for tales of shadows and songs she'd sing,
Elizabeth Charmer, a name still dear,
the pride of Ludlow's yesteryear.

May Fair

It was just for one night
the fair was coming to town.
Ferris wheels and roundabouts in full flight,
sweet smells of toffee apples and candy floss
wafting through the air.

Coconut Shy aim for the target!
Boys and girls having fun,
fairground music very loud,
screams and laughter from the crowd.

Everyone a winner for one night
hoopla, roll a penny, throw a dart,
beat the man in the fight.
Tomorrow it will all be a different sight.

From The Harbour

Sitting in the harbour,
taking in the view,
Cadair Idris holds its beauty
as the breakers unfurl
against the wide expanse
of golden beach,
boats bobbing, fishermen
remove their catch.

Barmouth nestled beside the
beautiful Mawddach Estuary,
calling you to explore.
Focus eyes to the left,
see the train appear
over the majestic bridge,
holidaymakers cheer.

Smiles from Davy Jones' Locker,
people taking lunch,
Knickerbocker ice cream
further up the street,
Take a moment, pop inside
the Sailors' Institute, seafarers'
stories to be told.

Walk through the steep,

winding streets of the town,

step away from shops,

walk the gorse-covered hills

of Dinas Oleu, ascending to

dramatic views, the

Mawddach Estuary, Cardigan Bay,

an artist's dream to display.

Moon On Water

One of these days, he won't beat me.
I watch every night
well, give or take the weather.
He looms over the sea,
roughing up the tides,
pulling at what he can.
Animals become unbalanced,
plants are confused
when fullness appears.

I know he will be full on tonight,
a warning to avoid a row
with my Emilia.
I'll make a wish and play safe,
be positive maybe I won't tell her?
I think she may guess,
as I won't be in full dress.

On The Edge

Standing on the edge,
today I face defeat,
feeling my heart miss a beat,
water, water at my feet.

Not today a lake or pond;
today it's the sea I've come to meet.
Screams of fear, profoundly deep,
water, water at my feet.

White horses rolling high,
frothy waves a battle cry,
gushing past, the water cold,
water, water at my feet.

People watching get a fright,
as white horses roll into sight.
They stand and stare at what they see,
water, water getting deep.

Look out to sea, what can that be?
A dolphin, graceful, leaping free.
Then down it floats upon the tide,
rising on white horses it sings a high note.

Gaze up above, dark clouds surround;

dolphin moves with a piercing sound,

leaving all around spellbound.

An orca rises with a frown,

water, water… I fear I'll drown.

The Passing Of Time

Glittering, shimmering all is flat.
Only two sounds: the waves that splash,
In the distance, the rumble of a train.

Forward he steps, already choosing the spot,
Inspecting the grain between his fingers,
The look on his face, shows delight.
No need for TV or laptop.

Looking out at miles of sand,
The work begins, his muscles flexed.
Hear the cogs whine and vibrate,
Ideas he puts into action.
Deep in thought, he knows what's next.

Build it up, windows, doors, turrets strong,
A moat deep and wide,
Winding trench to catch the tide.
Look at his watch; it won't be long.

Moving fast, boy backs it to the hilt,
Placing driftwood, shells and flag.
Stands back to watch the sea move in,
Believing dreams can be built.

(Observation Of My Grandson Jack, Aged Six Years Old, On Barmouth Beach, By Our Caravan.)

I Saw Red

Amongst the crowd, I saw sadness,

individuals remembering

lives that had gone before;

mutterings of stories being told.

I smelt the fear of what they represented,

the beauty of what they respected.

A sea of red flowing through the land.

Now safe in my home,

I hold one that will never leave me.

**(Installation of poppies, 2014, Tower of London "Blood Swept
Land and Sea of Red.")**

Rain On The Window Pane

Let me explain
how the rain
can entertain.
It runs down the pane
as fast as a train.

The children can see
what magic can be
when indoors they stay,
when it's too wet to play.

Choose a raindrop
it starts at the top,
races down the window pane,
keep in the lane

Ready To STOP!

Snowdrops

Slender you stand in the frozen snow,

Never ceasing to amaze how you survive,

Obeying the wintery whispers as you grow.

Wondrous woodland bloom,

Delicate petal bells the changes ring,

Ring out winter, welcome spring.

Occupying the covered ground,

Pious sisters, heads bowed in prayer,

Share the beauty, silence abound.

Daffodils

I took a walk down memory lane,
it didn't look the same.
The street looked bare,
no one to call or care.

In my thoughts, I hear the neighbors talk,
kids were playing games with chalk.
The windows shone, nets were white,
flowers grew; what a beautiful sight.

Now all I can do is stand and stare,
bricks and rubble everywhere.
Where have all the nice folks gone?
Walk on by and carry on.

Then on rocky ground,
three lonesome daffodils I see.
I'll pick them for Nelly
I know she won't have any.

Walk into the churchyard,
I know she will be there.
I'll place the flowers on her grave,
Only she knows I care.

Chocolate Delight

If I were a chocolate bar,
what would I be?
Fruit and Nutty Cadbury's large,
or Ferrero Rocher, yes by far.

Mars, strip off the layers,
delightful, erotic, and smooth.
Take your time and enjoy,
poor old teeth, it will destroy.

Now, if Bounty is your fave,
dream of relaxing on a beach,
mouth-watering coconut,
what a treat.

Come take a Picnic,
enjoy it anywhere,
crispy, wafer, chewy, crunchy,
peanuts, if you dare.

If I were a Cadbury's little egg,
I'd give my friends a treat.
Air-fry me in pastry,
Now this you cannot beat.

Unravel

Like a ball of wool
dropped from the armchair,
carefully rolling along
the floor; shapes, twirls,
patterns unravel a story.

The beginning starts at
my feet, looping smoothly,
as the years unfold,
weaving and rotating,
crossing over paths
I've trodden before.

Time never stood still,
some big twists and turns,
some sharp bends, hills
and dales taken in my
stride. No breaks,
until the end.

Writers Task

I picked up a poetry book,
I read the contents page.

I knew at once I'd get stuck.
I selected five titles.

I said, "they appealed to me,"
I knew the planning was vital.

I had to edit, by changing adverbs,
I edited more by giving it rhythm.

I felt my brow develop a frown,
as I looked at Maggie's Sonnet Four.

I did try to complete the task, knowing
I wouldn't obtain a decent score,

I'm giving up!
And watching Channel 4.

I'm Lost

Lost in the woods and full of doubt,
the sun obscured by overgrown trees;
a tangled track, no gate to be seen.

Just how long I wandered,
testing each brambly path, silent pleas,
waiting for guidance to be shown.

Wandering clumsily, fraught and fatigued,
I took refuge to ponder:
could this day go on much longer?

At first I was astounded,
what troubles brought me here?
Swiftly, a change of wind
took away my fear.

Lifting the veil,
I exhaled
and suddenly it was all so clear.

I had a choice to make today:
take the path away from the shadow.
Now I see my way.

First Thoughts

I feel fuzzy, it's dark
well, it would be;
my eyes are shut tight.
I know something is about
to happen, but it won't
register yet.

I hear the neighbour
set off to work,
is he in Birmingham
or Hull today?
Not my business;
it's too early yet.

I fear to stir,
hesitate what day is it?
What fate may unfold today?
Dare I take a peek at the
curtain left with a chink?
Roll over still time to think.

I put my nose
outside the duvet
as the comforting
waft of toast floats up the stairs.
My tummy settles today, Tuesday:
writers group; share our views.

Seven days still in
my week, how lucky
I am to have my senses
and friends to wake up to.
I will be more gracious and
meet each morning,
dance on the morning dew.

(AIM: Get To Bed Early)

Start And End In A Box

Three score and ten years that's me.

"Snug as a bug," Mum told me, in my small box, as a bab. Life was that way till I was five; snug. Then the changes, ups and downs till I got a job.

Had a few chaps, lots of rock 'n' roll. One or two heartbreaks, till I found my mate. Then our two girls. One of them had a boy, then a girl; my life can now live on.

A book of snaps, a life of love.

The big box won't be as snug.

Choices

Put the cards on the table,
toss a coin.
Stop at the signpost
time moves too fast.
Make up your mind:
decide now or never.

Thinking… or is it too late?
Which road to take?
Be real, or leave it to fate?
Always questions maybe
sometimes debate.

This time be fearless;
life has no guarantees.
Out of your comfort zone,
seek the mysterious unknown.
It may not be easy
but you won't be alone.

What Do I Know?

In the grand scheme of things,
I know nothing,
the older I get,
the less I know.
The kids say,
"what do you know?"

The girl at work
is having an affair.
I don't want to know.
Who knows what tomorrow
will bring?

This moment
I know the grass is green,
the sky is blue.
I can see it's still me
in the mirror.

This moment
I know I have a family
I can see,
and I know them
by their names.
Do I need to know more?

Just in Case, Dilemma

I'm going to a ball next month,
it's a black tie do.
Need another dress,
last year's just won't do.
I've sent for one from the internet,
black with a Brigitte Bardot neck.
I could borrow my daughter's,
that would hit the spot.

The one from the internet, sits
just below my knee.
Might not be suitable
for all to see.
I've got a silver necklace,
it really is quite bold.
Would it be suitable
for a Bardot neck?
It's really quite sweet,
it would look neat,
but too much leg
could look cheap.

Now the one I could borrow,
the one that fits all,
the one that's very sleek,
goes right down to my feet.
It has a cross-over back.
Can I go without a bra?
Send for some special aids,
they are meant to do the trick.
Tick the box, add them
to the basket,
they should come quick.

I'm off out tonight,
black tie do.
Cross-over dress, perfect.
Bra cups, I threw.
Now I'm going braless,
and I've got no stress.

The Fork In The Road

Put the cards on the table,
toss a coin.
Stop at the signpost,
time moves too fast.
Make up your mind,
decide now or never.

Thinking, is it too late?
Which road to take?
Be real or leave it to fate?
Always questions, maybe.
No time to debate.

Chance to be fearless,
life has no guarantees.
Out of your comfort zone,
seek mysteries unknown.
The road won't be easy,
but you won't be alone.

While I'm Young

Now I'm a young woman, I shall wear white,
without a hat but with extensions in my hair,
and I shall save my wages for holidays, a sports car,
and spa weekends, and I will buy a Help to Buy ISA.

I shall join a gym and stay fit,
and dine on lettuce and green tea,
and abseil and run a marathon,
and raise a glass of bubbly to the old folks
who wished they had, but didn't.

I shall buy Jimmy Choo shoes,
and have an AstroTurf lawn,
and sit and enjoy gossip.

You can look smart in designer gear and stay fit,
and join me on my five a day,
or a curry treat on Friday night,
and recycle our rubbish into the appropriate bins.

It is fun being young, exploring the world together.
I just need it to go on forever.
Be like my gran and break all the rules,
but never wear purple.

The Old Chocolate Box

I've got a lovely chocolate box,
it belonged to my gran.
She gave it to my mum.
Gran said, "it came from Stan."

Stan was her first love,
he was a lovely man.
He brought her the chocolates in the box,
that is when love began.

Stan went away to war,
he wrote letters to my gran.
All were stored in the box.
He wrote a wedding plan.

Stan never did come back.
The box had a church on the lid.
My mum and I smile.
Nan fell in love with Sid.

LOST YEAR

A child lay on his comfy bed,

put his thoughts on his pillow,

put shattered dreams out to nowhere.

He was lost, not a mate in sight.

He ached for the freedom stolen from him.

Sounds of nothingness echoed loud and clear.

With the loss of real communication came fear.

On the pillow the boy placed

what had happened during lockdown,

things he wanted to do with his life.

He did not understand this pandemic,

Who put it there like a bolt in the night.

Those he loved spoke of distancing,

putting a space between.

He got up, washed his hands,

this was the start.

He left his mark on his pillow,

went down to the computer screen.

This is Zooming madness for a child

who should be out in the park.

His chin held in his hands,

he looked at his screen.

He could feel his heart beating

and the soft breeze in his hair.

His feet tingled with excitement of movement.

On the screen it told him

the vaccine would give freedom.

His bubble soon burst.

The Image

No longer does the tree sway,
I no longer have a home.
Safer near the ground today,
my image dropped from the sky.

As it grew wiser and older,
its beauty changed its form.
No longer standing bolder,
dry dust and bark now keep
the ground warm.

**(Inspired By A Photograph Taken By My Then Eight-Year-Old
Granddaughter, A Fallen Tree, Part Of Which Gave The Image Of
A Bird)**

A Selection Of Haiku Poems

Rolling thunder crash
Lightning bright in the night sky
Rain pitter-patters

Ebony night sky
Rolling thunder crashing roars
Flash lightning rain, rain.

Rain stops, sun comes out
Steam rises from the damp lawn
Wiggly worm pops up.

Survivors step out
Bodies lie beneath the sea
Lost souls journeys end.

Orangium

It gave me an idearium,
When they said you didn't rhyme,
But if my orangium has rhythm,
What does it tiddlirum?

If I can roll you faster,
Slower, hiddlyum and biddlyum,
I know we'll start a
Fan crazycum.

The kids will all cum a run a jump,
What the heck, you don't rhyme,
And when the game, kumpa hump,
Weems all going to do a pith a ton.

When all the playing's done,
We'll call a trucy juicy,
Juicy Lucy, squeeze teazy,
Orangium unrhyming jabberwocking fun.

My Hobby

Ukulele, U3A that's the place to be,

Keep strumming, play the chords

Under the Boardwalk; sing the song

Learn the tempo, get the rhythm

Ensemble gather, upbeat genre

Lift the spirit, lots of fun

Enjoy entertaining, patience is the key.

WATCH OUT!

Full moon in the sky

Dark clouds gliding by

One black cat and many bats

Make an eerie silhouette

Not the night for wandering pets

The witches cast their spells

The sorcerer has no regrets.

Superstitions

Oh, how I wish the black cat
Up the street,
Would cross my path and
Bring me luck, then a
Pound, I would pick up.

I could hear the siren screaming
Along the road,
Now how difficult with my
Heavy load, cross my fingers,
I was told.

Cross my fingers, whatever
I was doing,
Never uncross, until you spot
A four-legged animal,
Only then were you safe.

Don't walk under a ladder,
My mother would scream,
WHY?
My brother anguished
When the window cleaner came,
Dripping wet one day
He got his answer.

I'd rather stay on the side of
Caution,
Bury a broken mirror, throw
Salt over my left shoulder,
If I spill any.

Call me crazy, if you please,
I know when I'm lucky,
Hunting for four-leaf clovers
To keep in my purse, happy
Pastime, sharing my luck
With friends.

FEAR

The smell of death, no child should face,
No mother, father, family dear,
Be forced to hold their hand to guide
To chambers dark and cold,
Death was forced upon these souls.

Do we learn from vicious men?
So evil they leave their mark.
Look around your world today,
With downcast eyes,
Do we need to pray?

For shame in hearts,
Atrocities, still go on today!

HOPE

Hope is a vessel
That quenches my thirst
Gives me time to think.

The sweetest taste,
Bitter thoughts,
Hope cannot be bought.

My empty cup,
Now filled with hope,
Wait till the storm is past.

Silent Fears

You may have stood next to me?

You thought, I was no different to you?

Did you feel my fear?

You didn't hear my silent cry?

Take a moment, I might have needed you,

I hide my fears.

Selfish

There's a word called selfish,
It means, I put me first,
I don't consider you,
Mine's an unquenchable thirst.

What is best for me,
Is all I care about.
I won't accept the consequences,
Infuriating, hurtful for others; no doubt.

(There's a lot of not very nice stuff going on around the world at the moment; and it's basically down to selfish egocentric people — this is my take on those people.)

Connection

She walks towards him,
He lifted his head,
His ears shot forward,
He could hear her heart
Beating, as she strode
Towards him.

Calmly she spoke to him,
Stroked his ebony coat,
They dispelled each other's
Fears. The partnership was
Strong. She found her
Teacher, to learn love
And connection.

He gives her healing,
Solace for body, soul
And mind. She leads
Him, he trusts her,
She never asks for more.

Purrfect Companion

While you sleep,
I hear your contented purr,
Whiskers twitch, snuggled in your
Favourite spot, I see the gentle rhythm
Of your heartbeat, pumping
Beneath your vibrant coat.

Peaceful cadence in your slumber,
I almost see you smile,
Remembering your tormenting
Play, before you captured
Your daily prey. Nature
Can be very cruel, when
You present me with your catch.

Now you stir, give a wide yawn,
Open eyes to hypnotize, then,
Start to preen; a yoga pose
I admire; now arch spine gracefully,
Reaching front paws upwards,
Flexible balance, I cherish
Your every move.

Slowly blink at me, a 'cat kiss,'
Of trust, intertwining between
My legs, groom my arm with
Your rough tongue, trilling and meowing
A soft happy sound, follow
Me around, I know you understand.

CAPTURED

Who would live in a comfy blanket,
Far from the maddening crowd,
I am at one wrapped up snug
Sitting on the seashore,
Listening to the tide
Pouring back through shingle,
Gulls fly, loud cries shouting
Through the sky.

Who would live and wake
To a new dawn,
Taste salt around their lips,
Feel the soft breeze and the
Breakers spray,
Rejoice as the dolphins
Frolic and sway.

Who would live with joy
Of memories, walking along
The pebbled shore,
White horses riding the waves,
Booming sounds crashing
Around the rocky caves.

Who would live and take solitude
At nightfall with stillness,
Calming sea, full moon beam
Rays down
Pool of silver;
Above, as if for me shooting stars appear.

(Enjambment Poem — Run One Line To The Next)

Don't Take It For Granted

Snaking around in the shimmering grass,
A snake is happily gloating,
Until the hawk passes.

Snugly Queenie, nesting in the woody patch,
Sisters supporting a motherly dream.
Obligingly, the babies hatch.

Caterpillar chooses the greenest leaf.
Butterfly emerges from the chrysalis,
Caterpillar's life is very brief.

Crickety, rackety, tappety,
Night time wooing mates,
Soothing humans, slumber happily.

Earthworms humbly sustainably,
Engineering through the soil,
Contributing to the world advantageously.

Busily buzzing, honeybee,
Waggle dancing forager,
Children spooning for their tea.

Humans guilty of many facts,
Boggling thoughtlessness
Of mankind's destructive acts.

Keep the earth green,
A responsibility we must all implore,
To prosper, thrive, and still be seen.

No Words

I'm hearing your screams
I'm hearing your pain
I'm hearing rapid noises in your brain
I'm hearing burning words
I'm hearing, confusion and fear
I'm hearing silent thoughts
I'm hearing words, you need to say
I'm hearing blue light,
I'm hearing, 'why me.'

I listen for signs of
silence, I listen for quiet
healing,
I listen for your peacefulness,
I listen for words of
understanding, I listen for peace
in body and soul, I listen for joy,
I listen for words of forgiveness,
I listen for my name,
I listen for a door to open,

Walk with me again.

Chocolate - Acrostic

Can you enjoy chocolate, and not put on weight?

Heaven no, that is testing fate -

Offer me a Chocolate Orange, Oreo, or Quality Street,

Calorie counting, no fun when a day's work is done,

Oh dear, I know I'll regret it, life is so bitter sweet,

Love it, but always share, that way it's more fun,

Always remember, chocolate is not a healthy treat,

Taste, smell, feel it smooth,

Enjoy your chocolate, but it can be cruel.

- (Acrostic poem)

Weather World - Acrostic

Wet and windy, puddles to splash,

Enchanting skies, 'old wives tales,'

Atmosphere to change our mood,

Time and seasons roll on by,

Hazy summer days, to laze away,

Excited children snowball fight, all day,

Rainbows bend across the sky.

Scorpio - Acrostic

Scorpio my star sign,

Cora is my name,

Observer of people, my claim to fame,

Resourceful, determined and mysterious,

Passionate, unwavering focused on goal,

Impossible to understand,

Once a friend, always a friend.

- Acrostic poem – my star sign

www.ingramcontent.com/pod-product-compliance
Lightning Source LLC
Chambersburg PA
CBHW051236120626
46547CB00013B/1671